# High-Interest/ Low-Readability Today's Far-Fetched News

## Ten Fables & Folktales Rewritten as High-Interest Front Page News Articles with Comprehension Activities and Audio CD

by
Sherrill B. Flora
and
Jo Browning-Wroe

**Today's Far-Fetched News**
Fables & Folktales

Front Page Story No. 5 *(The Ugly Duckling)*          Today's Date

### The Ugly Duckling is Back in Town— and He's a Hunk!

Last year, we told the sad story of the Ugly Duckling. All his life, the farm animals had told him he was too big and too ugly.

His upset mother said, "I tried to make them stop teasing him. But, it was no good. He got sick of it and now he's gone."

A year later, we can now tell you, the Ugly Duckling is back! And he's not ugly and he's not a duck!

KE-804066 © Key Education   -22-   Today's Far-Fetched News—Fables & Folktales

**Today's Far-Fetched News**
Fables & Folktales

Front Page Story No. 8 *(Jack and the Beanstalk)*          Today's Date

### Rare Beanstalk Bites the Dust!

Today Jack and his mother faced the angry town. For the last six months a rare beanstalk has grown in their front yard. Many people had come to love the plant.

Buses full of people have come from miles around just to see it. But not any more. Last night Jack and his mother cut down the beanstalk.

KE-804066 © Key Education   -39-   Today's Far-Fetched News—Fables & Folktales

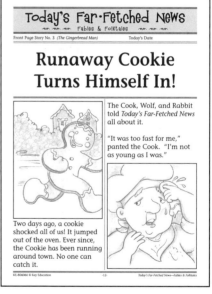

**Today's Far-Fetched News**
Fables & Folktales

Front Page Story No. 3 *(The Gingerbread Man)*          Today's Date

### Runaway Cookie Turns Himself In!

The Cook, Wolf, and Rabbit told *Today's Far-Fetched News* all about it.

"It was too fast for me," panted the Cook. "I'm not as young as I was."

Two days ago, a cookie shocked all of us! It jumped out of the oven. Ever since, the Cookie has been running around town. No one can catch it.

KE-804066 © Key Education   -13-   Today's Far-Fetched News—Fables & Folktales

illustrated by
Julie Anderson

**Publisher**
Key Education Publishing Company, LLC
Minneapolis, Minnesota

www.keyeducationpublishing.com

## CONGRATULATIONS ON YOUR PURCHASE OF A KEY EDUCATION PRODUCT!

The editors at Key Education are former teachers who bring experience, enthusiasm, and quality to each and every product. Thousands of teachers have looked to the staff at Key Education for new and innovative resources to make their work more enjoyable and rewarding. Key Education is committed to developing and publishing educational materials that will assist teachers in building a strong and developmentally appropriate curriculum for young children.

### PLAN FOR GREAT TEACHING EXPERIENCES WHEN YOU USE
### EDUCATIONAL MATERIALS FROM KEY EDUCATION PUBLISHING COMPANY, LLC

**Credits**
**Authors:** Sherrill B. Flora and
     Jo Browning-Wroe
**Art Director:** Annette Hollister-Papp
**Illustrator:** Julie Anderson
**Editor:** George C. Flora
**Production:** Key Education Staff
**Broadcasters on Audio CD:**
   George and Sherrill Flora

Key Education welcomes manuscripts
and product ideas from teachers.
For a copy of our submission guidelines,
please send a self-addressed,
stamped envelope to:
**Key Education Publishing Company, LLC**
**Acquisitions Department**
**9601 Newton Avenue South**
**Minneapolis, Minnesota 55431**

### About the Author of the Stories:

Jo Browning Wroe has taught both in the United Kingdom and in the United States. She earned her undergraduate degrees in English and Education from Cambridge University, Cambridge, England. She worked for twelve years in educational publishing before completing a Masters Degree in Creative Writing from the University of East Anglia, Norwich, England. Most of her time is now spent writing teacher resource materials and running workshops for others who love to write. Jo has been the recipient of the National Toy Libraries Award. She lives in Cambridge, England with her two daughters, Alice and Ruby, and her husband, John.

### About the Author of the Activities:

Sherrill B. Flora is the Publisher of Key Education. Sherrill earned her undergraduate degrees in Special Education and Child Psychology from Augustana College and a Masters Degree in Educational Administration from Nova University. Sherrill spent ten years as a special education teacher in the inner city of Minneapolis before beginning her twenty-year career in educational publishing. Sherrill has authored over 100 teacher resource books, as well as hundreds of other educational games and classroom teaching aids. She has been the recipient of three Director's Choice Awards, three Parent's Choice Awards, five Teacher's Choice Awards, and six Creative Child Magazine Awards. She lives in Minneapolis, Minnesota with her two daughters, Katie and Kassie, and her very supportive husband, George.

Standard Book Number: 978-1-602680-42-5
*High-Interest/Low Readability:*
*Today's Far-Fetched News*
Copyright © 2009 by Key Education Publishing Company, LLC
Minneapolis, Minnesota 55431

# Introduction

## About the Stories

The stories and activities found in *High Interest/Low Readability: Today's Far-Fetched News* have been specifically designed for students who are reading below grade level; for students who have reading disabilities; and for students who are reluctant or discouraged readers.

The engaging stories are written between early-first grade and early-third grade reading levels. Each story's specific reading level and word count can be found above the story title on the Table of Contents (page 4). This information should help guide the teacher in choosing stories that are appropriate for the individual needs of the students. *(Reading grade levels are not printed on any of the stories or on any of the reproducible activity pages.)*

The stories are printed in a large, easy-to-read font. Struggling readers are often intimidated and easily overwhelmed by small print. The larger font, picture clues, and sentence structure should help children feel more confident as they read the articles included in *Today's Far-Fetched News*.

All of the stories use high-frequency words and essential vocabulary. A list of the story's high-frequency words, as well as the special words that are necessary for each story, are found on pages 61 and 62. Prior to reading a story, review the word lists and introduce and practice any unfamiliar words. Make flash cards of the new words and outline each letter with glitter glue to provide a tactile experience for the students. Draw a picture of the word on each card to help students visualize any new vocabulary.

## About the Audio CD: *Today's Far-Fetched News*

Each story comes with its own evening news broadcast and begins with a few seconds of introductory music. Following the music, the news anchor welcomes the listeners and says, "Tonight's headline story is. . .. " That is the student's clue to listen. The news anchor reads the headline title and the content of the story exactly as it is printed on the student's copy of the news article.

For many struggling readers, being able to listen to the story first can be extremely beneficial. Knowing the story's content ahead of time provides students with the opportunity of using context clues to help decode words and for interpreting the meaning of the story. For other students, being able to track the text as they listen to the words allows for a beneficial multi-sensory experience. Students can hear the words; see the words; and they can touch each word as they follow along listening to the evening news broadcast.

## About the Activity Pages

Paper and pencil tasks are often "not fun" for struggling readers. The majority of the reproducible activity pages are divided into two different activities per page. The teacher may choose to assign both halves at once. The diversity of the two different activities should encourage the children to finish the page and not become bored or frustrated. The teacher may also choose to cut the page in two and assign each half at different times.

Coloring, drawing, solving puzzles, and cutting and pasting activities have been included. These types of activities reinforce a wide range of reading skills and are often viewed as "more fun" by the students.

In short, *High Interest/Low Readability: Today's Far-Fetched News* will provide your students with a complete reading experience.

# Contents

# Ants Give Grasshopper a Job!

Two weeks before Christmas, the ants gave Lazy Legs Grasshopper a job! Ants know how to be kind. Ants know how to work hard!

Lazy Legs upset the ants last summer. He told them to chill out. He said they should enjoy life more. He sang a rude song about them.

In his song he sang that ants never had any fun. All ants ever do is work hard to get food for the winter.

When asked why the ants gave Lazy Legs the job, the ants said, "It's a win-win! Lazy Legs gets money for food and we get to hear his music. Lazy Legs may be rude (and lazy), but oh, can he sing!"

Name ______________________________

*Complete Sentences*

**Directions:** Choose the correct word from the Word Bank to complete each sentence.

| **Word Bank:** | **work** | **winter** | **sing** | **food** | **job** |
|---|---|---|---|---|---|

1. The ants gave Lazy Legs Grasshopper a ______________________ .
2. Lazy Legs Grasshopper can______________________very well.
3. Lazy Legs Grasshopper does not like to ______________________ .
4. Ants work hard to get ______________ for the ______________ .
5. Do you think Lazy Legs Grasshopper will work hard with the ants?

   Why or why not? ______________________________________

______________________________________________________

*Creative Writing*

**Directions:** Create an advertisement to get more worker ants. It will be printed in *Today's Far-Fetched News.*

Name _____

**Directions:** Read and then cut out the sentences at the bottom of the page.
Glue them under the correct picture.

The ants work hard.

The ants give the grasshopper a job.

Lazy Legs is lazy.

Lazy Legs can sing.

# Gary Goat Beats Fred Fox in Court!

Gary Goat has won his case against Fred Fox.

"I am so happy," said Gary.

"Fred played a mean trick on me. I was stuck down in that well for days. Now, he has to pay!"

Last summer, when Fred Fox fell down a well, he asked Gary Goat to join him. He tricked Gary. He said the water was good to drink. It was very cold.

So, Gary climbed down into the well. Then, Fred got on Gary's back and climbed out. Now, poor Gary was the one left down in the well.

Fred Fox said, "No hard feelings. I hope Gary will come to my party. There will be a lot of fun and food."

Gary left with Fred. Let's hope Gary knows what he's doing.

Name _____

**Directions:** Look at each of the characters. Write a list of words that would describe each of them.

| Gary Goat | Fred Fox |
|---|---|

Name _____

**Directions:** Choose the correct word from the Word Bank to complete each sentence.

| **Word Bank:** food fox well back goat fun party |

1. Gary is a _____ .

2. Fred is a _____ .

3. Gary was stuck in a _____ for days!

4. Fred climbed on Gary's _____ to get out of the well.

5. Fred is going to have a _____ !

6. Fred said, "There will be a lot of _____ and _____."

---

*Creative Writing*

**Directions:** Draw a picture of Gary Goat and Fred Fox. Write a sentence about them.

# Runaway Cookie Turns Himself In!

The Cook, Wolf, and Rabbit told *Today's Far-Fetched News* all about it.

"It was too fast for me," panted the Cook. "I'm not as young as I was."

Two days ago, a cookie shocked all of us! It jumped out of the oven. Ever since, the Cookie has been running around town. No one can catch it.

"I'm young," said the Wolf. "But, it was too fast for me."

"I'm very fast, but not that fast," said the Rabbit.

Late last night, the Cookie called us from a secret phone number.

"I felt I was born to be wild. It was such fun. But now, I know I was born to be eaten," the Cookie told us.

The Cookie asked *Today's Far-Fetched News* to find a nice child who loves to eat cookies.

It could be you! Write to *Today's Far-Fetched News* and tell us why you should be that child.

## I should get to eat the cookie because:

_____

_____

_____

_____

_____

_____

_____

_____

_____

_____

Name_____

**Directions:** Cut out the cookie puzzle pieces and glue them together in the box.

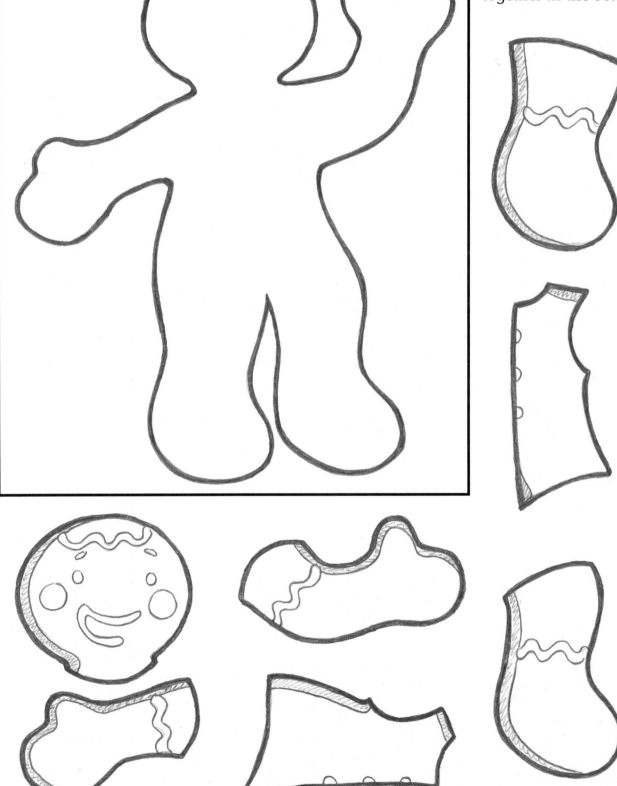

**Directions:** Read the question in each box. Write your answer in each speech bubble.

1. What do you think the Cook is saying to the Cookie?

2. What do you think the Cookie is saying as he runs away?

3. What do you think the Rabbit is yelling to the Cookie?

4. What do you think the Cookie is saying?

Name_____

**Directions:** Draw a picture of a different cookie. Wite a sentence about your cookie.

```
┌─────────────────────────────────────────────┐
│                                               │
│                                               │
│                                               │
│                                               │
│                                               │
│                                               │
│───────────────────────────────────────────── │
│- - - - - - - - - - - - - - - - - - - - - - - -│
│───────────────────────────────────────────── │
└─────────────────────────────────────────────┘
```

*Cloze*

**Directions:** Choose the correct word from the Word Bank to complete each sentence.

**Word Bank:** eaten   catch   called   wild   wolf   jumped   cook

1. The Cookie _____ out of the oven!

2. No one could _____ the Cookie!

3. The _____, _____, and Rabbit could not catch the Cookie.

4. The Cookie _____ from a secret phone number!

5. The Cookie wanted to be _____ !

6. But, cookies should be _____ !

# Today's Far·Fetched News

## Fables & Folktales

# Don't Panic –
# It's Not the End of
# the World!

Yesterday afternoon, Chicken Little ran into our news room. She looked very afraid. "The sky is falling! A chunk of it hit me on the head," she yelled.

Her friends, Goosey Loosey and Henny Penny told us, "It's true! We saw the mark on her head! The sky is falling!"

We ran Chicken Little's story. The town is now in a panic. The stores have no food. No one has gone to work. The children have not gone to school.

Everyone has dug big holes in their yards. They're hiding in the holes— waiting for the sky to fall.

But then, early this morning, Chicken Little came back to the news room.

"I was wrong," she said. "An acorn hit me on the head. It wasn't the sky after all. I don't know what came over me. Maybe I've watched too much TV. Sorry. You can all go back to work now."

But can we? We just hope that everyone will come out of their holes and read this paper. If not, they could be hiding in their holes a long time!

Name _____

**Directions:** Read each sentence about the story. Write a "**T**" on the blank if the sentence is true. Write an "**F**" on the blank if the sentence is false.

1.  Chicken Little said, "The sky is falling!" _____

2.  Henny Penny and Goosey Loosey did not see the mark on Chicken Little's head. _____

3.  The town was in a panic. _____

4.  Everyday the children went to school. _____

5.  The people hid in the holes that they dug in their yards. _____

6.  An acorn hit Chicken Little on the head. _____

**Directions:** Pretend you are a reporter for *Today's Far-Fetched News.* What two questions would you ask Chicken Little?

1.

2.

Name_____

**Directions:** Choose a word from the Word Bank to answer each crossword question. Write the answer in the correct word boxes.

**Word Bank**

Loosey    Chicken    sky

Penny    nut    Little

| **ACROSS** | **DOWN** |
| --- | --- |
| 3. _____ Little | 1. Chicken _____ |
| 4. An acorn is a _____. | 2. "The _____ is falling!" |
| 6. Goosey _____. | 5. Henny _____ |

Name_____

**Directions:** Look at the pictures at the bottom of the page.
Cut them out along the dotted lines and glue them in the correct order.

| | |
|---|---|
| 1 | 2 |
| 3 | 4 |

# The Ugly Duckling is Back in Town— and He's a Hunk!

Last year, we told the sad story of the Ugly Duckling.  All his life, the farm animals had told him he was too big and too ugly.

His upset mother said, "I tried to make them stop teasing him. But, it was no good. He got sick of it and now he's gone."

A year later, we can now tell you, the Ugly Duckling is back! And he's not ugly and he's not a duck!

We asked him why he came back to the farm today.

"I wanted to see Mom and tell her I'm ok," he said.

When asked if she was glad to see him, his mother said, "Oh yes! He may be a big swan movie star, but he will always be my little ducky."

"It turns out I was a swan," said the hunky bird today. "I didn't look like the other ducks because I wasn't one!"

We asked him if he was angry with his brothers and sisters.

"Sure, they gave me a hard time, but I'm ok now. After all, I'm the one with all the chicks chasing me! I'm a model and I'm making lots of money. I'm about to make my first movie."

Name _____

**Directions:** Write answers to the following questions.

# Why did the Ugly Duckling run away?  Why did he come back?

**Directions:** Circle **yes** or **no** for each sentence.

1. The Ugly Duckling is really a duck.                          **yes**     **no**

2. The Ugly Duckling is going to be in a movie.                 **yes**     **no**

3. The Ugly Duckling is really a swan.                          **yes**     **no**

4. The Ugly Duckling wants to live on a farm.                   **yes**     **no**

5. The Ugly Duckling is angry with his brothers
   and sisters.                                                 **yes**     **no**

6. The Ugly Duckling's mother calls him "my
   little ducky."                                               **yes**     **no**

Name_____

**Directions:** Read and then cut out the sentences at the bottom of the page.
Glue them under the correct picture.

| The Ugly Duckling did not look like his brothers. | The Ugly Duckling will be in a movie. |
| The Ugly Duckling is a model. | Mother Duck loves the Ugly Duckling |

Name_____

**Directions:** Create a movie poster for the Ugly Duckling's first movie.

*Word Search*

**Directions:** Circle the words from the Word Bank in the word search.
The words may be horizontal or vertical.

| t | j | k | v | p | s | l | u | c | e | m |
|---|---|---|---|---|---|---|---|---|---|---|
| d | u | c | k | l | i | n | g | n | x | o |
| x | e | b | d | i | s | g | l | m | z | t |
| o | t | p | r | e | t | t | y | d | c | h |
| s | w | a | n | c | e | x | w | b | h | e |
| e | f | v | f | a | r | m | x | i | x | r |
| b | r | o | t | h | e | r | l | g | e | r |
| c | r | k | z | s | m | o | v | i | e | w |

### Word Bank
duckling
mother
swan
ugly
movie
sister
brother
farm
pretty
big

# Chef Leaves Town— Takes Magic Stone with Him!

Last night, the people of Main Street ate the best meal of their lives.  At six o'clock in the evening, a man was walking down Main Street. He knocked on all the doors! He was asking for food.

"We don't have any extra food," said Mr. Cant. "We are not mean. We just do not have any food to spare. And, it's not very polite to be asking for food."

"He said he was making Stone Soup, so I gave him water," said Mrs. Smith. "And he just dropped the big stone in it."

"Then, he said a bit of salt would be good, so I gave him salt," said Mr. Jones.

The stranger had picked a bad day. No one on Main Street had any food to share. He should have left town, but he didn't. Instead, he did a strange thing.

Right there in the street, the man got out a pot. Then, he lit a fire. Soon, the people of Main Street all came out of their homes. They wanted to see what this man was doing.

"And I got him a carrot," said Miss Lee. "And Mr. Cant gave him a potato. Mrs. Buck gave him a cabbage. And Mr. Long gave him some beef."

"It was very mean of him," said Mrs. Smith. "He gave us a taste of heaven and then he took it away from us."

"That's right," said Mr. Jones. "We will never be able to eat that soup again!"

If any of our readers know of a good soup recipe, please send it to *Today's Far-Fetched News!*

"It was the best soup I had ever eaten," said Mrs. Smith.

Everyone thought the stone must have been pure magic.

But today, the people of Main Street feel let down. The new chef seems to have left town. And even worse, he took the magic stone with him.

**Recipe Card**

Name of Soup:

Ingredients:

What you do:

Name_____

**Directions:** A **fact** is something that is true. An **opinion** is something that a person thinks, believes, or feels. Write the word "**fact**" or the word "**opinion**" next to each sentence.

_____ 1. A man knocked on all of the doors on Main Street.

_____ 2. The people said they did not have any extra food.

_____ 3. The strange man was very hungry.

_____ 4. The stone was magic.

_____ 5. The strange man cooked a very good soup.

---

*Creative Writing*

**Directions:** Pretend you are a reporter for *Today's Far-Fetched News.*
What two questions would you ask the stranger with the stone?

1.

2.

Name_____

**Directions:** Look at the town. Circle the following items: carrot, celery, chicken, potato, onion, salt, pepper, water jug, and pot.

*Cloze*

**Directions:** Choose the correct word from the Word Bank to complete each sentence.

| **Word Bank:** | knocked | pot | lit | food | carrot | beef |
|---|---|---|---|---|---|---|

1.  The strange man asked the people if they had any extra _____.

2.  The strange man _____ on many doors.

3.  The strange man put a _____ in the middle of the street.

4.  The man _____ a fire under the pot.

5.  Miss Lee gave the man a _____.

6.  Mr. Long gave the man some _____ .

**Directions:** The **main idea** tells what the story is about. Read the following sentences and circle the sentence that you think best explains the main idea of the story.

1.  The people of Main Street will learn how to cook.

2.  A stranger tricks the people of Main Street into giving him food so he can make the soup!

3.  Magic stones make really great soup.

**Directions:** **Antonyms** are two different words that have the opposite meaning. For example, "up" and "down" are antonyms. Draw a line from each word in **Column A** to its matching antonym in **Column B**.

| Column A | Column B |
| --- | --- |
| empty | pretend |
| cold | good |
| near | hot |
| real | woman |
| man | full |
| bad | far |

# What a Waste! Three Wishes and Nothing to Show for it!

Last night, John and Jean Chopper made the biggest mistake of their lives.

John, a wood cutter, told *Today's Far-Fetched News*, "It's not an easy life. Cutting wood is hard work and the pay isn't good. But all that could have changed. If only we had been smart."

John told us his story. "I was about to chop down a big tree when this funny little guy popped out of the tree trunk. He begged me not to cut down his tree.

There were lots of other trees for me to cut down, so I didn't cut down his tree."

"Is that when he gave you three wishes?" we asked.

John answered, "Yes. Then, he popped back into the tree."

John went home and told his wife the good news. And this is when it all started to go wrong. Jean gave John a glass of soda pop. John took a sip of it and then wished, (yes, wished!), that he had a hot dog to eat with it.

"That was not very smart, John," we said.

John replied, "It sure wasn't! But that's not the end of it. We did something else."

"We sure did," added Jean. "I was so mad at him for wasting a wish, I said I wished, (yes, wished!) that the hot dog would stick to his nose. And it did! The hot dog was stuck on John's nose!"

"Now, we only had one wish left," said John.

"If we had left the hot dog on John's nose—we could have wished for lots of money. But would you like to spend your life with a hot dog on the end of your nose?" asked Jean.

"I wouldn't," our reporter said.

"And neither would I," said John with a sad smile.

"So, we wished for the hot dog to come off his nose—and it did," said Jean.

"And then we drank our soda pop and ate the hot dog—which was very good by the way," said John.

Readers, if you were given three wishes, what would they be? A hot dog and a soda pop? Don't think so! Write to us at the newspaper and we'll print your wishes.

## My "3" Wishes

Name _____

**Directions:** Look at the pictures at the bottom of the page.
Cut them out along the dotted lines and glue them in the correct order.

| | |
|---|---|
| 1 | 2 |
| 3 | 4 |

Name_____

**Directions:** Choose a word from the Word Bank to answer each crossword question. Write the answer in the correct word boxes.

## Word Bank

three    wishes    hot

man    John    Jean

### ACROSS

3. _____ was a wood cutter.

5. John was given _____ wishes.

### DOWN

1. John had three _____.

2. A little _____ jumped out of a tree.

3. _____ is John's wife.

4. John had a _____ dog stuck to his nose.

Name_____

**Directions:** Read the question in each box. Write your answer in each speech bubble.

1. What do you think the little man is saying to John?

2. What do you think John is saying to Jean?

3. What do you think Jean is saying to John?

4. What do you think John is saying to Jean now?

# Rare Beanstalk Bites the Dust!

Today Jack and his mother faced the angry town. For the last six months a rare beanstalk has grown in their front yard. Many people had come to love the plant.

Buses full of people have come from miles around just to see it. But not any more. Last night, Jack and his mother cut down the beanstalk.

Mr. Green, a world expert on beanstalks, said, "How could they have done such a thing? There has never been a beanstalk like it. It has made our town famous! It was rare! It was lovely! And now, it is dead." Mr. Green looked like he might cry.

"You silly little man," said Jack's mother. "We had to cut it down! A man-eating giant would have been running around town. He would have been yelling, 'Fee Fi Fo Fum, I smell the blood of an Englishman.'"

Jack's mother added, "How would you have liked that? You'd be in his big fat tummy by now. So, don't tell me I did anything wrong!"

Mr. Green said, "I'm not here to talk about giants. I'm here to talk about beanstalks. I'm here to stand up for their rights. I'm here to speak for all the plants that can't speak for themselves!" Again, Mr. Green looked like he might cry.

It's not just the plant lovers who are upset with Jack and his mother. The Mayor sent them a letter this morning. Jack's mother told us what the Mayor wrote.

"The Mayor said it doesn't look good to have a dead giant in your front yard. He said it looks messy. He said if it isn't gone by the end of the day, we will have to pay a fine. Does he think that we want a dead giant in our front yard? Trust me, we don't. But, he's so big! How will we get rid of him?"

We asked Jack's mother, "What are you going to do?"

"Start digging a very big hole, I guess," she said.

Today, this story took another turn. Just before *Today's Far-Fetched News* went to print, Jack came into the news room. He gave us a slip of paper and asked us to put it in today's paper.

On the paper was written: **For Sale. One Magic Bean. Will sell to the highest bidder.**

Name_____

**Directions:** A **cause** tells why something has happened and an **effect** tells what happened. Draw a line from each cause in **Column A** to its matching effect in **Column B**.

<table>
<tr><td><u>Column A</u></td><td><u>Column B</u></td></tr>
</table>

1. The rare beanstalk helped to make,

2. If the beanstalk had not been cut down,

3. Mr. Green almost started to cry,

4. The Mayor wrote Jacks's mother a nasty letter,

a. the giant would have come to town and scared all the people.

b. to make her remove the giant from her yard.

c. the town famous.

d. because he wanted the plant to live and grow.

---

**Directions:** Read each question. Circle the picture that answers each question.

1. Who cut down the beanstalk?

3. Who wanted to save the beanstalk?

2. Who fell from the beanstalk?

4. Who had one more bean to sell?

Name _____

**Directions:** Look at each of the pictures. Write a sentence about what you think is happening next to each of the pictures.

**Directions:** Circle the words from the Word Bank in the word search.
The words may be horizontal or vertical.

b x b c w y p g q
e x c m a y o r s
a q l J t v d o l
n g i a n t c w p
s r m c u f e l l
t e b k m a i l a
a e m o t h e r n
l n l l q w x v t
k q g l y a r d s
n e w s p a p e r

**Word Bank:** beanstalk    giant    green    yard    mayor
Jack    fell    plant    mother    newspaper    grow    climb

Name_____

**Directions:** Cut out the giant puzzle pieces and glue them together in the box.

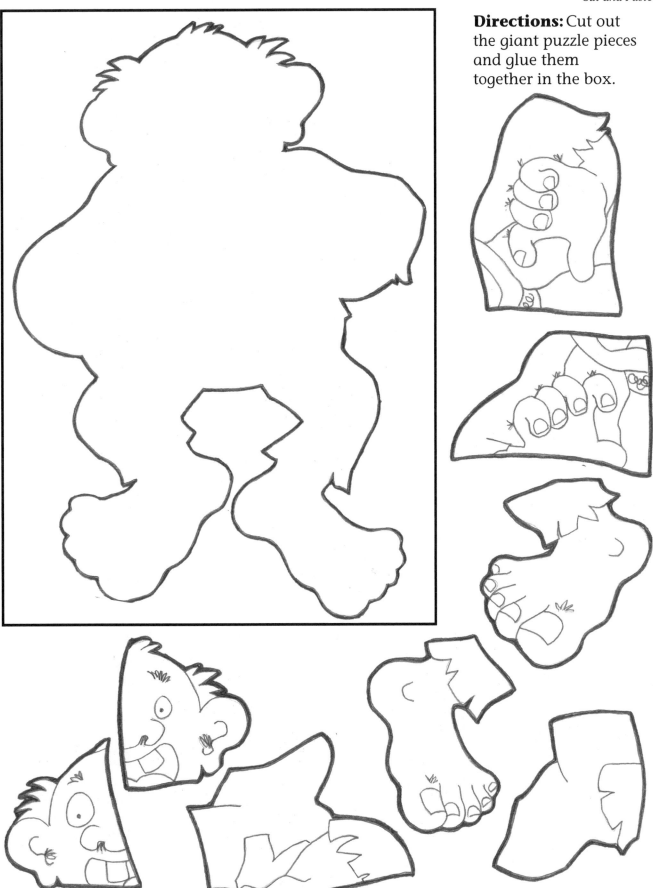

# Today's Far·Fetched News

## Fables & Folktales

# Troll Butted Off Bridge by Gruff Brother!

Last night, a fight broke out on the bridge.  The oldest Gruff brother butted the Troll with his horns.  In the first of two reports on this story, Mira Mouse writes:

From his hospital bed, the Terrible Troll said, "It's my bridge!  Everyone knows if they cross it, I will eat them. Who does that Goat Gruff think he is?"

"The whole town says he's a hero," said Mira Mouse.

"They do?" asked the Troll.

"They say it's only fair that everyone can cross the bridge," stated Mira Mouse.

"Really?" grumbled the Troll.

"Yes. The whole town has now crossed the bridge. There's a big party in the field."

The Troll yelled, "I'm a troll. It's my job to be mean! It's my job to eat people. Isn't it?"

Mira said, "You could try being kind."

"Don't trolls have to be nasty?" asked the Troll.

"Who says Trolls have to be nasty?" Mira asked.

"In all of the stories, trolls are mean," said the confused Troll.

"You could be the first nice Troll," said Mira.

We think Mira from *Today's Far-Fetched News* has made the Troll think.

Roly Rat has been at the party over the bridge. This is his report:

Until yesterday, no one went near the bridge. Today, people ran over it! They danced over it! They skipped over it! This is the biggest party the town has ever seen.

The Gruff brothers looked like movie stars. Everyone wanted to have their pictures taken with the goats. I asked the brothers to tell their story.

"After a dry summer, there was no grass on our side of the bridge. We had to go over the bridge. We were hungry," said Sam, the smallest brother.

"We were sick of the Troll," said Mark, the middle brother. "We had a right to go over the bridge."

"So, we came up with a plan," said Gary, the oldest and biggest Gruff brother. "My brothers would go over the bridge one at a time. They would tell the Troll there was a bigger goat coming. They'd say, don't waste your time on us. I was sure I could push him off the bridge."

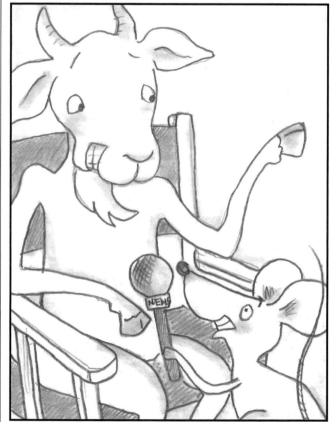

"That was very brave, Gary," Roly said.

"Not just Gary," butted in Sam. "I was the first to go over the bridge. I was scared. He might have eaten me!"

Roly asked, "When did you plan this?"

Sam answered, "We had the idea about a month ago. But Gary had to work out first. He had to be in great shape. We helped him train."

"And it paid off," said Gary, looking very proud.

A doctor at the hospital has just spoken to *Today's Far-Fetched News*. She said that the Troll will be able to go home in three days.

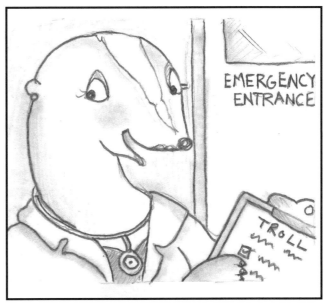

When we asked how he was, the doctor said:

"He seems to be confused. He can be nice and kind. Then, he can be very rude. He told me he was going to eat me. Then he asked me how to make friends."

We will have to wait and see. Will the Troll try to be nice? Will he share the bridge? Write and tell us what you think will happen.

**Will the Troll try to be nice?**
**Will he share the bridge?**
**What do you think?**

_____

_____

_____

_____

_____

_____

_____

_____

_____

_____

_____

_____

_____

_____

_____

_____

_____

Name_____

**Directions:** This is the bridge in the story. Read each sentence and then follow the directions.

1. Draw an "O" on the biggest goat.
2. Draw an "X" on the little goat.
3. Color the Troll green.
4. Color one mouse gray.
5. Color the other mouse blue.
6. Color the cat orange.
7. Color the pig pink.
8. Color the duck yellow.
9. Color the trees green.
10. Color the bridge brown.

Name_____

**Directions:** Read the words at the bottom of the page. Which words describe the Troll? Which words describe the biggest Gruff brother? Which words can be used to describe both of them. Cut out the word boxes along the dotted lines and glue them into the correct section of the Venn diagram.

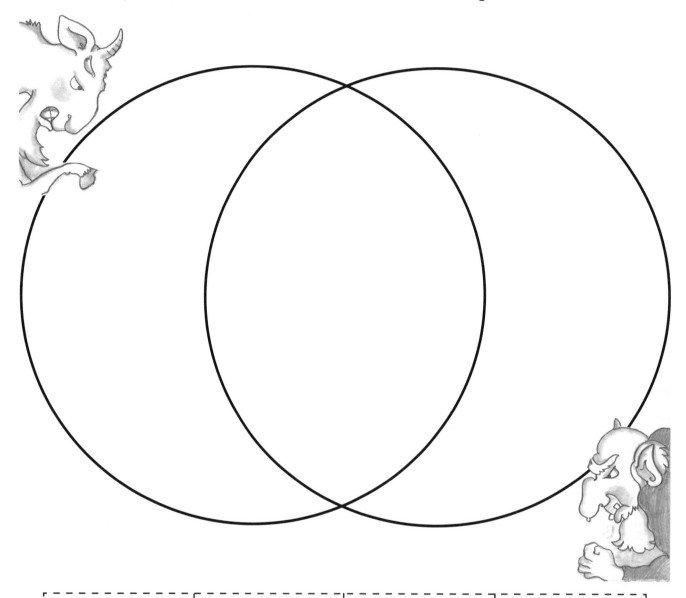

| | | | |
|---|---|---|---|
| 4 legs | mean | likes the bridge | got into a fight |
| 2 legs | nice | in the hospital | has 2 brothers |

Name _____

**Directions:** Choose the correct word from the Word Bank to complete each sentence.

| **Word Bank:** party three nice rat under mouse pushed |
| --- |

1. The Troll lived _____ the bridge!

2. There were _____ Gruff brother goats!

3. Mira is a _____ and Roly is a _____.

4. Gary Gruff _____ the Troll off the bridge.

5. Mira tried to talk the Troll into being _____ .

6. There was a _____ in the field!

---

**Directions:** A **cause** tells why something has happened and an **effect** tells what happened. Draw a line from each cause in **Column A** to its matching effect in **Column B**.

### Column A

1. When the Troll was pushed off the bridge,

2. With the Troll in the hospital,

3. The Troll told the people he would eat them if they tried to walk over the bridge,

4. After the doctor talked with the Troll,

### Column B

a. so no one in the town ever walked over the bridge.

b. he wanted to know how to make friends.

c. he ended up in the hospital.

d. the people could safely walk over the bridge.

# Today's Far·Fetched News
## Fables & Folktales

# Jack's House to be Knocked Down!

The town is in shock!  Jack is going to knock down his house. Mrs. Maiden, who lives next door, told *Today's Far-Fetched News:*

"All of us who live on the street are very upset. It won't be the same without The House that Jack Built."

Jack spends most of his time alone.  At last, he agreed to talk—but only to *Today's Far-Fetched News.*

"I've had it," he told reporter Mira Mouse.  "I'm sick of the questions."

"What questions?" Mira asked.

"I'm sure you can guess," said Jack.

"Ahh, no," answered Mira.

"Stop messing with me, Mira.  You know all about the questions," said Jack.

"I'm not messing with you, Jack. What questions?" asked Mira.

Jack went on to say, "Let's say I gave you a snack."

Mira liked that idea. "That would be great, Jack. I'm hungry."

Jack replied, "No! I'm saying IF I gave you a snack. Maybe a snack with some cheese."

Mira giggled and said, "I'd say, great Jack! I love cheese! I am a mouse after all."

Jack yelled, "No you wouldn't, Mira! You would ask me one of the questions! You would say, Tell me, Jack, is this the cheese that lay in the house that you built? Then, you'd look at the floor and say, Oh! I think I just saw the rat that ate the cheese that lay on the floor of that house that you built."

Mira said, "Jack, I don't know what you are talking about!"

Jack shouted, "Yes, you do! Everyone knows. Then, they would spot my cat, and they would ask, say Jack, is that the cat, that killed the rat, that ate the cheese that lay in the House that you built?"

Mira was very confused now. She said, "Why would they ask that?"

"Because of the poem!" said Jack. "The poem that made my house so famous."

In a very quiet voice, Mira said, "Well, I don't know the poem."

Shocked, Jack said, "Yes, you do!  Next, you would see the dog next door, and you would ask me if that was the dog, that worried the cat, that ate the rat...blah blah blah."

Mira squeaked, "But, I don't see any dog next door.  And if did, I wouldn't ask you about it."

Jack went on saying, "Then, you would hear a cow and you would say, hey Jack, is that the cow with the crumpled horn, that tossed the dog, that worried the cat... blah, blah, blah."

"Oh Jack, can we talk about something else?" asked Mira. "Like where are you going to live?  Will you build a new house?"

Jack said in a stern voice, "I know what you really want to ask me. You want to know where IS the maiden who was all forlorn, that milked the cow with the crumpled horn...blah, blah, blah."

Mira replied, "No, I don't! Jack, do you want to know the truth? I'm bored with your poem.  I don't know your poem. I don't care about the cheese, the rat, the cat, the dog, the cow, or the maiden!"

"Oh, my! What a shock!" said Jack. "You really don't know my poem, do you?"

"No Jack, I really don't," said Mira.

Now, Jack looked upset. "That's bad! That's really bad. I thought EVERYONE knew the poem about 'The House that Jack Built.'"

"Well, Jack, I'm proof that they don't," said Mira.

Jack said, "I can't knock down my house now. Not until everyone knows the poem."

"But, you said you were sick of it. That's why you wanted to knock the house down," said Mira.

As it turned out, Jack thought everyone knew the poem. He looked at Mira and said, "Sit down, Mira, I've got something to show you. This is the cheese…"

*Today's Far-Fetched News* is sorry to say that Mira Mouse did not stay for the rest of the poem. She ran screaming from the house.

*Today's Far-Fetched News* has printed Jack's poem on the next page. We thought some of our readers (like Mira) might not know it.

# THE HOUSE THAT JACK BUILT © 1878

This is the House that Jack built.

This is the cheese,
That lay in the House that Jack built.

This is the Rat that ate the cheese,
That lay in the House that Jack built.

This is the Cat that killed the Rat,
That ate the cheese,
That lay in the House that Jack built.

This is the Dog that worried the Cat,
That killed the Rat,
That ate the cheese,
That lay in the House that Jack built.

This is the Cow with the crumpled horn,
That tossed the Dog,
That worried the Cat,
That killed the Rat,
That ate the cheese,
That lay in the House that Jack built.

This is the Maiden all forlorn,
That milked the Cow with the crumpled
    horn,
That tossed the Dog,
That worried the Cat,
That killed the Rat,
That ate the cheese,
That lay in the House that Jack built.

This is the Man all tattered and torn,
That kissed the Maiden all forlorn,
That milked the Cow with the crumpled
    horn,
That tossed the Dog,
That worried the Cat,
That killed the Rat,
That ate the cheese,
That lay in the House that Jack built.

This is the Priest, all shaven and shorn,
That married the Man all tattered and
    torn,
That kissed the Maiden all forlorn,
That milked the Cow with the crumpled
    horn,
That tossed the Dog,
That worried the Cat,
That killed the Rat,
That ate the cheese,
That lay in the House that Jack built.

This is the Cock that crowed in the
    morn
That waked the Priest all shaven and
    shorn,
That married the Man all tattered and
    torn,
That kissed the Maiden all forlorn,
That milked the Cow with the crumpled
    horn,
That tossed the Dog,
That worried the Cat,
That killed the Rat,
That ate the cheese,
That lay in the House that Jack built.

This is the Farmer who sowed the corn,
That fed the Cock that crowed in the
morn,
That waked the Priest all shaven and
    shorn,
That married the Man all tattered and
    torn,
That kissed the Maiden all forlorn,
That milked the Cow with the crumpled
    horn,
That tossed the Dog,
That worried the Cat,
That killed the Rat,
That ate the cheese,
That lay in the House that Jack built.

Name_____

**Directions:** Read each sentence about the story. Write a "**T**" on the blank if the
sentence is true. Write an "**F**" on the blank if the sentence is false.

1.  Mira Mouse is a reporter for *Today's Far-Fetched News.*          _____

2.  Everyone knows the poem, "The House that Jack Built."          _____

3.  Jack had a new house, so he didn't need his
    old house anymore.          _____

4.  Jack wanted everyone to know the poem about his house.          _____

5.  Mira Mouse wanted to buy Jack's house.          _____

6.  Jack decided not to knock down his house.          _____

---

**Directions:** The **main idea** tells what the story is about. Read the following sentences
and circle the sentence that you think best explains the main idea of the
story.

1.  Everyone should know the poem, "The House that Jack
    Built."

2.  Mira was learning about all the things that you can
    put in Jack's big house.

3.  Mira was talking with Jack to find out why he wanted
    to knock down his house.

Name_____

**Directions:** Pretend you are a reporter for *Today's Far-Fetched News.*
What two questions would you ask Jack?

## 1.

## 2.

**Directions:** Design a new house for Jack.

# High-Frequency, Easy-to-Sound Out, and Special Words for Each Story

| | | | | | | | |
|---|---|---|---|---|---|---|---|
| a | changed | field | hope | mark | please | snack | two |
| able | children | find | hot | may | poor | so | ugly |
| about | child | fired | house | maybe | pot | some | up |
| afraid | climbed | first | how | me | print | something | upset |
| after | cold | floor | I | meal | proud | son | us |
| again | come | food | idea | mean | push | song | very |
| all | coming | for | I'm | might | pushed | sorry | wait |
| alone | could | friend | in | miles | put | speak | walk |
| always | cross | from | into | more | question | spend | walking |
| am | crossing | full | is | morning | questions | stand | want |
| an | cry | fun | isn't | mother | ran | stone | wanted |
| and | cut | funny | it | much | read | stop | wants |
| animals | day | gave | it's | must | readers | stores | was |
| another | days | get | I've | my | reporter | story | water |
| answered | did | give | job | nasty | rid | street | way |
| any | dig | given | jumped | near | right | sure | we |
| are | digging | glad | just | needs | room | such | well |
| aren't | do | go | kind | never | run | takes | went |
| around | dog | going | know | new | running | talk | were |
| as | doing | golden | large | next | sad | talked | what |
| asked | done | gone | last | nice | said | tell | when |
| asking | don't | good | later | night | sale | than | where |
| at | door | got | lay | no | same | that | who |
| ate | down | great | left | nose | sang | the | wife |
| away | drank | guess | let | not | saw | their | will |
| back | drink | guy | lets | now | says | them | win |
| bad | dropped | had | letter | of | scared | themselves | wins |
| be | early | happen | life | off | school | then | window |
| bear | easy | happy | like | oh | see | there | wish |
| because | eat | hard | liked | oldest | seems | they | wishes |
| been | eaten | has | lit | on | sell | thing | with |
| bed | egg | have | little | one | send | think | without |
| before | end | haven't | live | only | sent | tired | wood |
| being | ended | he | lives | our | shape | this | work |
| best | even | he's | long | out | share | time | worse |
| big | ever | head | look | over | she | to | would |
| bigger | everyone | hear | looked | paper | should | today | write |
| biggest | fair | help | lot | party | shouted | together | writes |
| bit | fall | helped | loves | pea | show | told | written |
| bites | falling | her | mad | people | silly | too | wrote |
| broke | farm | here | made | picked | since | took | yards |
| but | fast | hiding | magic | picture | sing | town | yelled |
| by | fastest | him | make | plan | six | trick | yes |
| called | fat | his | makes | planned | skipped | tried | yesterday |
| came | feeling | hits | making | plant | sky | true | yet |
| can | fell | hole | man | play | slip | try | you |
| can't | felt | homes | many | played | smart | tummy | your |
| | | | | | | turn | you're |
| | | | | | smile | | |

# Special Words for Each Story

### Special Words for Story #1
ants
chill
Christmas
enjoy
grasshopper
Lazy Legs
money
music
rude
summer
*Today's Far-Fetched News*
win
winter

### Special Words for Story #2
beats
court
Fred Fox
Gary Goat
pay
summer
trick

### Special Words for Story #3
born
catch
cookie
himself
number
oven
panted
phone
rabbit
runaway
secret
shocked
town
turns
wolf
young

### Special Words for Story #4
acorn
afternoon
Chicken Little
chunk
Goosey Loosey
Henny Penny
panic
waiting
watched
world
wrong
yesterday

### Special Words for Story #5
angry
brothers
chasing
chicks
duck
duckling
ducky
hunk
hunky
model
movie
sisters
star
swan
ugly
year

### Special Words for Story #6
beef
cabbage
carrot
chef
evening
extra
knocked
leaves
magic
Main Street
Miss Lee
Mr. Cant
Mr. Jones
Mr. Long

Mrs. Buck
o'clock
potato
recipe
salt
soup
spare
stranger

### Special Words for Story #7
begged
Chopper
Jean
John
mistake
neither
newspaper
nothing
replied
soda pop
stick
trunk
waste
wished
wishes
woodcutter

### Special Words for Story #8
angry
beanstalk
bidder
blood
crowd
dead
dust
Englishman
expert
fee fi fo fum
front
giant
grown
highest
lovely
man-eating
Mayor
months
rare
tummy
world

### Special Words for Story #9
brave
bridge
brothers
butted
doctor
Gruff
grumbled
hero
hospital
Mira Mouse
nasty
Roly Rat
terrible

### Special Words for Story #10
blah
bored
built
cheese
confused
cow
crumpled
forlorn
horn
house
idea
Jack
knocked
maiden
messing
poem
questions
rat
reporter
stern
town

# Answer Key

**Top of page 6**
1. job;  2. sing;  3. work;
4. food / winter;  5. *answers will vary*

**Bottom of page 6**
*Check students' work*

**Page 7**
1. Lazy Legs is lazy.
2. The ants give the grasshopper a job.
3. Lazy Legs can sing.
4. The ants work hard.

**Page 10**
*Check students' work*

**Top of page 11**
1. goat;  2. fox;  3. well;
4. back;  5. party;  6. fun / food

**Bottom of page 11**
*Check students' work*

**Page 14**
*Check students' work*

**Page 15**
*Check students' work*

**Top of page 16**
*Check students' work*

**Bottom of page 16**
1. jumped;  2. catch;  3. cook, wolf;
4. called;  5. wild;  6. eaten

**Top of page 19**
1. T;  2. F;  3. T;  4. F;  5. T ;  6. T

**Bottom of page 19**
1. *check students' work*

**Page 20**
*Across:*  3. Chicken;  4. nut;  6. Loosey
*Down:*  1. Little;  2. sky;  5. Penny

**Page 21**

**Top of page 24**
*Check students' work*

**Bottom of page 24**
1. no;  2; yes;  3. yes;
4. no;  5. no;  6. yes

**Page 25**
1. Mother Duck loves the Ugly Duckling.
2. The Ugly Duckling will be in a movie.
3. The Ugly Duckling did not look like his brothers.
4. The Ugly Duckling is a model.

**Top of page 26**
*Check students' work*

**Bottom of page 26**
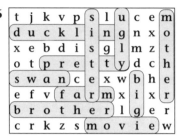

**Top of page 30**
1. fact;  2. fact;  3. opinion;  4. opinion;  5. fact

**Bottom of page 30**
*check students' work*

**Top of page 31**
*check students' work*

**Bottom of page 31**
1. food;  2. knocked;  3. pot;
4. lit;  5. carrot;  6. beef

**Top of page 32**
2. A stranger tricks the people of Main Street into giving him food so he can make soup.

**Bottom of page 32**
empty/full;  cold/hot;  near/far;
real/pretend;  man/woman;  bad/good

**Page 36**
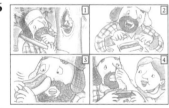

**Page 37**
*Across:*  3. John;  5. three
*Down:*  1. wishes;  2. man  3. Jean;  4. hot

**Bottom of page 38**
*Check students' work*

**Top of page 42**
1. c;  2. a;  3. d;  4. b

**Bottom of page 42**
1. Jack;  2. giant;  3. Mr. Green  4. Jack

**Page 43**
*Check students' work*

**Page 44**

# Answer Key

**Page 45**
*Check students' work*

**Page 51**
*Check students' work*

**Page 52**

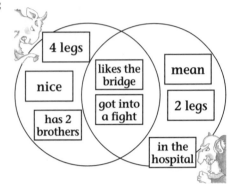

**Top of page 53**
1. under;  2. three;  3. mouse, rat;
4. pushed;  5. nice;  6. party

**Bottom of page 53**
1. c;  2. d;  3. a;  4. b

**Top of page 59**
1. T;  2. F;  3. F;  4. T;  5. F ;  6. T

**Bottom of page 59**
3.  Mira was talking with Jack to find out why he wanted to knock down his house.

**Top of page 60**
*Check students' work*

**Bottom of page 60**
*Check students' work*

---

## This book supports the NCTE/IRA Standards for the English Language Arts

Each activity in this book supports one or more of the following standards:

1. **Students read many different types of print and nonprint texts for a variety of purposes.** *Today's Far-Fetched News* includes 10 reading passages at varying reading levels, along with audio recordings of those passages to build both reading and listening skills.

2. **Students use a variety of strategies to build meaning while reading.** Comprehension activities focusing on drawing conclusions, main idea, sequencing, inference, and vocabulary, among other skills, support this standard.

3. **Students communicate in spoken, written, and visual form, for a variety of purposes and a variety of audiences.** Activities in *Today's Far-Fetched News* incorporate drawing and writing for a variety of purposes.

4. **Students use the writing process to write for different purposes and different audiences.** *Today's Far-Fetched News* includes writing activities focused on a variety of audiences and purposes.

5. **Students incorporate knowledge of language conventions such as grammar, spelling, and punctuation; media techniques; and genre to create and discuss a variety of print and nonprint texts.** Writing activities *in Today's Far-Fetched News* take different forms, from sentences to dialogues to advertisements, allowing students to practice different forms of writing and writing conventions.

6. **Students use spoken, written, and visual language for their own purposes, such as to learn, for enjoyment, or to share information.** The engaging stories in *Today's Far-Fetched News* will motivate students to read independently, and the skill-building activities will support students in becoming more effective independent readers and writers.

---